"This Inaugural Lecture—presented before a distinguished audience of thought leaders, policy makers, researchers, academics, and students—is inspirational, motivational, scholarly, well presented and organized (in a non-linear way), and contains a good balance of theory, policy, and realistic activism. The main text is presented together with two supplemental brochures that are beautifully crafted, aesthetic, content-oriented, highly informative, and enlightening."

— **Leonard G. Epstein**, former Senior Adviser on Culture, Language and Health Literacy with the Health Resources and Services Administration, United States Department of Health and Human Services

A New Narrative of Peace

The George and Lisa Zakhem
Kahlil Gibran Chair for Values and Peace
University of Maryland

A New Narrative of Peace

The Vision and Programs
of the Gibran Chair

Proceedings of the Inaugural Lecture by
May A. Rihani

Organized by
**The College of Behavioral and Social Sciences of the
University of Maryland**

and
**The George and Lisa Zakhem Kahlil Gibran Chair for
Values and Peace**

in association with
The Embassy of Lebanon in Washington, D.C.

20 SEPTEMBER 2016

Preface by
Wallace D. Loh

Remarks by
Gregory F. Ball
Ali Karanouh

A NEW NARRATIVE OF PEACE:
THE VISION AND PROGRAMS OF THE GIBRAN CHAIR

ISBN-13: 978-0-9983465-0-2
ISBN-10: 0-9983465-0-0

Suggested bibliographic citation for this publication:
    Rihani, May. *A New Narrative of Peace: The Vision and Programs of the Gibran Chair*. The proceedings of an Inaugural Lecture delivered at the University of Maryland on 20 September 2016. College Park, MD: University of Maryland, 2017.

Video excerpts from the Inaugural Lecture are available online at:
go.umd.edu/gibranlecture

Publication edited and produced by Michael Dravis,
University of Maryland

Book interior and cover designed by Nadim van de Fliert

For information about the George and Lisa Zakhem Kahlil Gibran Chair for Values and Peace, please visit: gibranchair.umd.edu

CONTENTS

FOREWORD

We live in a time that increasingly tests our values and commitment to peace. Waves of distrust and enmity slowly wash away the mutual respect that holds our communities together—here and abroad.

How fortunate, then, that the George and Lisa Zakhem Kahlil Gibran Chair for Values and Peace thrives at the University of Maryland. Few academic centers focus so tightly on values that can help to bridge cultural, religious, and national differences.

The new director of our Gibran Chair, May Rihani, comes singularly qualified to confront these challenges. She shares a similar background with Kahlil Gibran himself: emigrant from Lebanon to the United States; multi-lingual author published in Arabic and English; equally conversant with the cultures of the East and West; and a champion of universal values. Her uncle was a confidant of Gibran.

Ms. Rihani follows in the tradition of the Chair's founder, Suheil Bushrui, her former teacher and longtime friend. Professor Bushrui passed away in 2015 after a teaching career spanning more than sixty years. He built a devoted following on four continents through his dedication to cultural pluralism, human rights, and the role of the arts in strengthening these values.

In her inaugural lecture, Ms. Rihani builds on this tradition. She lays out steps that can strengthen the common core of values that bind communities. Focus on what we share, rather than what divides us, she says, drawing on her remarkable experience in fostering international development and education for women and girls. Even at a time of growing conflict, she reminds us that people have never given up their hope for peace.

I would like to thank the many individuals who have supported the Gibran Chair and its important work, most notably George and Lisa Zakhem. As Ms. Rihani puts it in her inaugural lecture, they are helping to write "a new narrative of peace for the twenty-first century."

Wallace D. Loh
President, University of Maryland
College Park, Maryland

President Wallace Loh opens the Inaugural Lecture proceedings by welcoming audience members to the University of Maryland. (Photo courtesy of UMD's College of Behavioral and Social Sciences)

ACKNOWLEDGEMENTS

This publication constitutes the proceedings of the Inaugural Lecture of the George and Lisa Zakhem Kahlil Gibran Chair for Values and Peace held at the University of Maryland (UMD) on September 20th, 2016. The Lecture took place under the distinguished auspices of Dr. Wallace Loh, President of the University of Maryland, and Dr. Gregory Ball, Dean of the College of Behavioral and Social Sciences (BSOS) at UMD.

I must thank both President Loh and Dean Ball for their continuous and generous support of the Gibran Chair and for their wise guidance. In particular, I would like to thank President Loh for providing the Foreword to this publication and also Dean Ball for serving as master of ceremonies during the Inaugural proceedings.

My gratitude goes to individuals from Dean Ball's office who lent their skilled assistance to the Inaugural Lecture event, especially: Sarah Goff-Tlemsani, Michelle Slone, Djuana Joseph, Laura Ours, and Andrew Roberts. Also, my thanks go to Gibran Chair staff Poupak Moallem and Nadim van de Fliert, both of whom worked tirelessly to ensure the success of the event.

I am also very thankful to the diligence, dedication, and professionalism of the team who put this publication together: Michael Dravis masterfully produced the publication by collecting the various elements, editing and proofreading them, and putting them together in a workable sequence. Nadim van de Fliert applied both a practical and artistic eye to the design of the covers and interior.

Laura Ours took photographs and supervised the video and audio recording of the proceedings. Janelle Thompson and Mona Rezvani were both diligent in helping to produce this publication; the former transcribed the speeches of President Loh and Dean Ball, and the latter assisted with proofreading and formatting.

I would be remiss if I failed to express my deepest thanks to my fellow speakers: President Wallace Loh, Dean Gregory Ball, and Mr. Ali Karanouh, representing the Embassy of Lebanon in Washington, D.C. Their speeches and presence gave a special ambience to the Inaugural Lecture.

In addition, I would like to thank the many professors, international development experts, professional colleagues, friends, and acquaintances who kindly took the time to send me written comments about the Inaugural Lecture. I wish we had the space to publish all the messages that were received; however, based on the advice of the publication's Editor, we selected a number of messages and have included them as an appendix.

May A. Rihani
The George and Lisa Zakhem Kahlil Gibran Chair for
Values and Peace
University of Maryland,
College Park, MD

Inaugural Lecture
Proceedings

Dr. Gregory Ball, Dean of the College of Behavioral and Social Sciences, delivers introductory remarks. (Photo courtesy of UMD's College of Behavioral and Social Sciences)

Introductory Remarks

Gregory F. Ball
Dean of the College of Behavioral and Social Sciences

I am pleased to introduce today's Gibran Chair Inaugural Lecture that will be presented by the new director, May Rihani. Why is the Gibran Chair for Peace and Values so important to the University of Maryland? Universities, especially research universities, are often subject to very intense criticism. Even though I dearly love universities and think the United States has some of the greatest universities in the world, which it absolutely does, we somehow have trouble making everyone happy. People are always pointing out that we do not do enough teaching, or that the teaching we do is not of the right type; or they might say that we do too much research, or that the research we do is not on the right topic.

In this context, one of the criticisms that comes forward is that universities have become too specialized and provide technical information in a dry context to enable students to pursue careers and drive the great engine of U.S. capitalism. Critics occasionally say, "Well, what happened to making students good citizens, broadening their understanding of the world, asking them to question what makes us human?" When people say that to me, I respond: "What you said has nothing to do with the College of Behavioral and Social Sciences here at the University of Maryland. Here, we do teach students about universal human values. We engage students in conversations about the complicated moral challenges faced by the world, and we integrate that into the curriculum in a very significant and important way." How do we do that? We do it in several ways, but one of the most important ways is through our three Peace Chairs.

1

When I was lucky enough to get the job as Dean of this College, one of the unique features to which I had to adapt as I had not been at a University with anything like them, was our Peace Chairs. There are three at Maryland: the Anwar Sadat Chair for Peace and Development held by Professor Shibley Telhami, the Bahá'í Chair for World Peace held by Dr. Hoda Mahmoudi—who is here today, I'm delighted to say— and finally the George and Lisa Zakhem Kahlil Gibran Chair for Values and Peace. All three of these Peace Chairs have goals that involve not only conveying knowledge to students and teaching courses and seminars in a traditional way, but also encouraging students to think in alternate, sometimes discomfiting ways. The Chairs challenge them to think about some of the major questions in the world including how our diverse peoples can work together, the problems humanity is facing and their personal roles in responding to them. Now, with each Chair, the Chairholder takes a particular perspective on these challenges.

In the case of the Gibran Chair, it is inspired by the life and writings of Kahlil Gibran, a true citizen of the world whose message of peace and love inspired whole generations in the West. He united the East and the West in a remarkable and figurative way with his writings, most notably *The Prophet*. I think it is safe to say—given the conflicts we face today in the world and public discourse between the East and the West— that we need the spirit and the writings of Kahlil Gibran more than ever. The tradition of this Chair was established by the late Professor Suheil B. Bushrui but he built a forum around his activities as Chairholder where everyone was welcome. All faiths—including atheists—were given a place at the table and were able to engage with each other in discussing the great challenges facing our society. As I faced the problem of how to possibly uphold this tradition as it is so unlike most tra- ditional academia, I was delighted when I was able to meet May Rihani and discuss her background, her interests and her

2

commitment. I knew that we had found the right person to carry on this tradition, so I could not be more pleased to echo President Loh's comments and to welcome May Rihani to the University of Maryland.

May will now present her Inaugural Lecture. As you probably know, May is from Lebanon where she received her education at the American University of Beirut. After she completed her graduate courses there, she came to the United States in the late 1970s and has pursued her career here ever since, although as she reminds me, she goes to Lebanon every year very faithfully, and stays in close touch with her homeland.

May, like Kahlil Gibran, is a citizen of the world. Her good works to change the world have touched people in all regions of the world; but I think especially in Africa. Recently, she served at the United Nations as Co-Chair for the UN Girl's Education Initiative. As reflected in her seminal book, *Keeping the Promise: A Framework for Advancing Girl's Education*, she has been instrumental in working in diverse cultures on how to change attitudes towards the education of girls and the empowerment of women so that their great talents can be tapped for the benefit of society.

May's combination of compassionate work and devotion to cultural scholarship makes her the perfect candidate to take over as the Director of the Chair. And so I am as pleased to welcome her, as I am to hear her give her Inaugural Lecture.

THE INAUGURAL LECTURE
A New Narrative of Peace:
The Vision and Programs of the Gibran Chair
MAY A. RIHANI

President Wallace Loh, Ambassador Massoud Maalouf, Dean Gregory Ball, Dean Bonnie Dill, Representatives of the Embassies of Lebanon, Tunisia, Qatar, Iraq, and Bahrain, distinguished colleagues, students, and friends;

It is my privilege to address you tonight about the critical issue of Peace, as the new Director of the George and Lisa Zakhem Kahlil Gibran Chair for Values and Peace.

Before I share some thoughts and reflections about Peace and my vision for the Gibran Chair, I would like to begin by acknowledging the important work accomplished by my distinguished predecessor, Professor Emeritus Suheil Bushrui, the Chair's first Director, and the person who set its course. Professor Bushrui was a visionary who worked tirelessly to enable his students and his colleagues, in fact all those whom he came in contact with, to become aware of the importance of that which connects all human beings. Although he described himself as "only a camel driver," Professor Bushrui recognized those essential elements which connect us and unify us, ultimately lead us to true and lasting Peace.

To follow the footsteps of such a visionary is challenging. However, being likewise inspired by the overpowering sense of our unity—which also inspired Kahlil Gibran—allows me to undertake the task with energy and gratitude.

Peace for Gibran emanates from his deep belief in the fellowship of humanity. He wrote:

5

I love you when you bow in your mosque,
kneel in your temple, pray in your church.
For you and I are sons of one religion,
and it is the spirit.[1]

Peace for Gibran is the result of a proactive approach that can make things happen. He wrote:

And all knowledge is vain save when there is work,
And all work is empty save when there is love;
And when you work with love you bind yourself to
yourself, and to one another.[2]

Gibran inspires, and that makes our work to build bridges to Peace a little easier.

Reflecting on Peace led me to recognize that global Peace is not only one of the greatest challenges of our modern world, but something that humanity has continually yearned for, despite its apparent elusiveness.

Peace has been central to human thinking and to the process of social and behavioral inquiry. Theories of Peace have been key to the study of conflict and wars, to the assessment of human aspirations and behaviors and to the understanding of the human mind.

In past centuries, Peace was examined based on many elements, situations, contexts, and conditions. Peace, conflicts, and wars were state-centric and were studied from the perspective of relations between sovereign states. Exploring and analyzing how states interact, what causes them to go to war,

---

1   Kahlil Gibran, *The Vision: Reflections on the Way of the Soul*, trans. Juan R.I. Cole (London: Penguin Books, 1998), 23.
2   Kahlil Gibran, *Gibran Khalil Gibran: The Complete Works*, comp. Tony P. Naufal (Beirut: Naufal, 2014), 79.

and what motivates them to seek Peace were key approaches to understanding what is at play.

Scholars who study Peace-making and Peace-building came to understand that Peace does not manifest itself only as the absence of war but as Spinoza wrote in 1670, "Peace is a virtue, a state of mind, and a disposition for benevolence, confidence, and justice."[3]

There are many schools of thought regarding the possibilities of achieving Peace. Among these schools that have emerged is the realist, or neo-realist school, which is pragmatic in its views. Kenneth Waltz wrote extensively about the neo-liberal school that views states as rational actors and the principal deciders between conflict or Peace. John Mearsheimer also writes extensively about this school of thought.

Other schools of thought include balance of power theory, liberal theory, economic interdependence theory, and several others.

The British theorist Paul Rogers offers an approach that is based on the fact that the central principles of Peace Studies allow it to remain flexible and evolve over time by embracing a "strong interdisciplinary outlook, a consciously global orientation, and a determined linkage between theory and practice."[4] I find my own thinking is very much aligned with Rogers's analysis.

Although Peace has been studied in the past, continues to be studied in the present, and will continue to be examined and analyzed, nonetheless, there are serious constraints and

3   Quoted in Thomas Gregory, *A Natural History of Peace* (Nashville, TN: Vanderbilt University Press, 1996), 4.
4   Paul Rogers, *Contemporary Security Studies* (Oxford: Oxford University Press, 2007), 68.

obstacles that muddle the pursuit to Peace, be it within each state, between states, or on the regional and global levels.

Research and analysis have shed light on the causes and characteristics of these obstacles; however, what has been researched and analyzed to date might not be enough to contribute to the advancement of Peace within each nation, between states, at the regional level, or globally.

Peace continues to be one of the greatest challenges because our global village, in this early part of the twenty-first century, is going through a period of acute turbulence. Wars, conflicts, divisions, and violence seem to be growing, economic inequality continues unresolved, and the tensions created by religion seem to be intensifying.

This elusive Peace that we all yearn for, despite all the obstacles that exist on the road towards it, is perhaps what is most needed in this century.

To understand further the prospects of Peace, policy makers, practitioners, academicians, and others must continue to unpack the possibilities of Peace, this very complex aspiration.

Because Peace is such a great challenge and yet so desperately needed, academicians, practitioners and decision makers should not relax but rather intensify efforts to study it. We should carefully consider how conflict can be avoided and how conditions for Peace be attained; how to build a new paradigm under which coming generations will value Peace and work to ensure that it can be obtained; how the voices of thought leaders and activists, who believe in the necessity of global and regional Peace, can be highlighted and underlined; and how through collaboration among academicians, practitioners, and decision makers, knowledge about the strategies that advance Peace can be enriched.

The Gibran Chair through its academic research and activities will contribute to this unpacking process of how to advance the understanding of and possibilities for Peace. The contributions of the Chair, though built on the results of past theoretical research, will be based on a strong interdisciplinary approach, and will be "consciously determined to find the linkages between theory and practice."[5]

The Gibran Chair will contribute to these efforts, starting with the acknowledgement that Peace is possible. We will dedicate our efforts to understanding the complexity of Peace and its realization.

With this overview in mind, I would like now to do four things:

- Share with you the vision of the Chair and the principles that will guide its programs;

- Discuss how the Gibran Chair will work and what its programmatic priorities are;

- Present what we hope the contributions of the Chair might be; and, then

- End this presentation with some reflections.

These topics are interrelated; therefore, my presentation will not follow a linear path.

The Gibran Chair is privileged to be housed in the College of Behavioral and Social Sciences, where interdisciplinary studies are natural and a matter of daily activities. An interdisciplinary approach will allow us to work with thinkers from different disciplines, both within the University of Maryland system

5   Ibid.

and with academicians from other institutions in the U.S. and abroad. Also, an interdisciplinary approach will facilitate our work with civil society leaders and organizations, as well as with policymakers. I believe that such collaborative efforts can result in the deepening of the understanding of Peace and in the possibility of advancing it.

I believe that the search for Peace will be an active process that may keep reinventing itself—adapting to circumstances and opportunities, and gaining more perspectives.

We will work in particular on deepening our understanding of how to help new generations understand that Peace is both possible and attainable. We will nurture the process of studying and exploring Peace with our students, just as we nurture any academic journey towards specific goals.

To advance its vision, the Gibran Chair's active programs will address major global topics, including:

- Studying the pursuit of Peace;

- Exploring paths towards Peace;

- Examining common ground;

- Understanding cultural pluralism;

- Highlighting the contributions of women to Peace;

- Deepening cross-cultural understanding;

- Transcending the so-called East is East and West is West barrier;

- Revisiting poetry, literature and art as connectors within the global village; and

- Celebrating universal human values.

The Chair's programs will be implemented in a variety of ways, including through: academic courses, research projects, lectures, seminars, workshops, symposia, conferences, and academic publications.

The Chair will celebrate people, events, and occasions that move Peace forward.

The list of what needs to be done is daunting; therefore, identifying principles that are the underpinnings of a realistic Peace is one of the major ways to advance effectively and efficiently.

Among the most prominent principles that will guide the work of the Gibran Chair are the following:

- Social justice as a foundational cornerstone of Peace;

- Inclusivity as a necessary condition to Peace; and

- Valuing diversity as a pathway to Peace.

And among the most relevant and pressing topics, given the state of our Global Village, are these:

- Improving and deepening understanding between the East and the West, or more specifically, between the ethos of the East and the cultural values of the West;

- Exploring how conflict, conflict resolution, Peace-building, and maintaining Peace involve, engage, and impact women;

- Examining how ensuring access to basic rights by everyone, particularly minorities and the underprivileged, reduces and hopefully eliminates many constraints and obstacles to Peace.

Based on the principles I just mentioned, I believe the vision for Peace in the twenty-first century needs to be a vision of social justice, a vision of inclusivity, and a vision that embraces all peoples.

The Gibran Chair will work independently and in collaboration with others to expand and deepen the research and analysis of the many facets of social justice and we are committed to working on several of its components. Through our Chair, social justice and Peace issues will be explored with insistence and persistence.

Our work on Peace will be based on a paradigm that includes a commitment to non-violent approaches, a behavior of non-discrimination, and a mindset that imbues every religion, every race, and every individual with respect—regardless of whether they are male or female, or belong to a majority or a minority.

As we work towards this vision of social justice, we will study and explore how we can:

- Strengthen commitments to resolving conflicts through non-violence;

- Increase the recognition that dialogue is a pathway to valuing others and acknowledging their rights;

- Reject simplistic conspiracy theories that purport to explain our problems and justify our malaise and ennui;

- Examine the assumption that most regional problems, and in particular global problems, cannot be resolved and Peace is totally illusive;

- Study success stories that illustrate that Peace is possible; and

- Engage in discourses that search for the common ground among cultures.

As we work towards this vision of deepening understanding among cultures, the Chair will engage in academic programs that explore how to bridge the traditional East-West divide. For example, next month under the Chair's auspices Dr. Maher Mahmassani will deliver a lecture entitled, "Secularism in Islam as a Path to Peace."[6]

The Chair will highlight the fact that a dialogue of civilizations is far more constructive and persuasive than the theory of a "clash of civilizations."[7] We need bridges not walls, and we definitely do not want battlements.

We work towards this vision of equality and inclusivity, we will study and explore how women can offer unique contributions to the Peace process, and how the perspectives of minorities are essential to reaching a sustainable Peace. In December, the Gibran Chair will conduct a one-day Symposium on "The Contributions of Arab Women towards a Lasting Peace." A dozen academicians and practitioners will participate with panelists from Lebanon, Syria, Egypt, Saudi Arabia, Tunisia,

---

6   Maher Mahmassani, "Secularism in Islam: A Path to Peace," lecture delivered under the auspices of the George and Lisa Zakhem Kahlil Gibran Chair for Values and Peace at the University of Maryland on 11 October 2016 (see go.umd.edu/Mahmassani).
7   See Samuel P. Huntington, *The Clash of Civilizations and the Remaking of World Order* (New York: Simon & Schuster, 1996).

Morocco, South Africa and the United States contributing to the discussions.

The presentations and discussions resulting from such programs will help break stereotypes that misinform us about each other. The Chair's activities will hopefully lead us to question our assumptions and arrive at understandings of that which we do not yet fully comprehend.

In addition to understanding the connections that link civilizations, the Gibran Chair recognizes the importance of exploring, through research, how Peace can be reached within different cultures, religions, geographic zones, and communities.

We will listen to, encourage and cultivate courageous ideas and actions, such as theological courage, or the courage to find positive and constructive interpretations of religions, and the courage to reject interpretations that lead to division, or the oppression of women, or the marginalization of the Other. The Gibran Chair will engage with scholars who write and publish, guided by the kind of theological openness that allows them to discover common ground among religions.

Through its activities and research, the Chair will pursue its commitment to finding effective ways of understanding and engaging others, and deepening respect for all cultures.

The Gibran Chair, like the other two Peace Chairs in our College of Behavioral and Social Sciences, will contribute to the reservoir of knowledge.

The Chair will help build a storehouse of knowledge of effective ways to break cycles of violence and promote a culture of non-violence as a path towards Peace.

We will contribute to the knowledge of students and communities, locally and globally, a knowledge that helps tip the scale against violence and towards Peace.

The Chair will examine if there is a body of knowledge that is based on a moral compass which acknowledges that social justice might be the safest and surest path towards nonviolent resolution of social and economic problems.

We will contribute to the knowledge that includes a value system that respects gender equality and recognizes that empowering women is in the interest of society as a whole.

Women can no longer be both half of the population and at the same time just an interest group. It pains me to observe that in many societies in our century, women and girls continue to be underserved and barred from decision making positions. It is time for us as a species to advance and step up to the level of basic equity.

The Chair will contribute to studies that recognize that protecting the rights of women and minorities, as well as underlining the enriching power of diversity, are among the surest roads to Peace.

In order to contribute effectively to such a body of knowledge, the Chair will work with researchers and activists on the importance of expanding their understanding of the power of active listening. Through active listening, the analysis of needs and situations becomes more accurate, and the possibility of empathizing with a variety of actors and situations leads to a recognition that human rights need to be granted to every individual regardless of race, religion, or gender.

The Gibran Chair will remain conscious of the fact that perhaps its greatest contribution will be to enhance opportunities for students and the younger generation to become visionaries and architects of a new narrative of Peace.

Perhaps the Chair could contribute to teaching new generations to permit themselves to dream about Peace, and to have the determination of positive thinking.

Perhaps, in collaboration with others, we will contribute to establishing a culture of thinking and reflecting about the possibility of solving problems without reverting to violence, of negotiating without ending that process too quickly, of attempting to reach a peaceful solution without ever giving up on that possibility.

The Chair will work with students on exploring a more detailed and more in-depth understanding of plural societies, and on the socio-cultural dimensions of human differences. We will conduct research that examines how to gain increased insights into cultural practices and cultural norms, and how to appreciate differences in these practices and norms. Also, we will suggest research that examines the process that facilitates the appreciation of these differences. The more we are able to appreciate differences and diversities, then the more we minimize the possibilities of conflict and maximize possibilities of finding roads to Peace.

Through research, academic courses, and advising and nurturing students, we will try to weave patterns of cultural connections.

The Gibran Chair will become an academic hub, an intellectual beehive, for professors and students alike, for researchers and activists, for individuals from the greater Washington area and globally. We are thankful that we enjoy such a powerful platform, and we will use it in the best way possible in the pursuit of Peace.

I invite students who are interested in exploring, research-ing, and creating new avenues in the pursuit of Peace, to con-tact the Gibran Chair so we can together pursue such impor-tant interests.

I invite researchers who are reflecting on and researching the different facets and strategies of Peace to contact the Gi-bran Chair so we can brainstorm together about next steps.

I invite other Chairs, departments, and professors who wish to collaborate on programs to advance Peace to get in touch with the Gibran Chair.

I invite leaders within civil society not to miss the oppor-tunity of contacting the Gibran Chair to investigate how this academic platform can be beneficial to civil society in the greater Washington area, but also to civil society in Lebanon, the birthplace of Gibran; in the Middle East, a region that is yearning for Peace; in Africa, a region with great promise; and of course globally.

►□◄

Although the Chair is not a large organization, it is part of a powerful university that shapes the minds of future gen-erations, a prestigious and powerful university that recognizes that with a young and promising generation we can find solu-tions to the complex problems of the world.

As Margaret Mead said:

> *Never doubt that a small group of thoughtful, com-mitted citizens can change the world, indeed, it's the only thing that ever has.*[8]

---

8   Quoted in Nancy C. Lutkehaus, *Margaret Mead: The Making of an American Icon* (Princeton, NJ: Princeton University Press, 2008), 261.

Gibran was not about closing doors, drawing boundaries, or building walls; on the contrary Gibran was about opening doors and windows and building bridges.

The more I reflect on the great contributions that the Gibran Chair can make, the more I imagine Gibran and the other thinkers and writers of the Arab Renaissance of the early twentieth century—such as Ameen Rihani and Mikhail Naimy—rejoicing in the fact that we are following in their footsteps. From my perspective, these thinkers from the geographically small country of Lebanon were the early globalists who brought the Arab world to the West, and the West to the Arab world. They were bridge builders. I see them as thought leaders who were able to transcend boundaries and barriers, and who understood how that which connects humanity is far more important and more significant than our differences.

These figures inspired many over several generations to build cultural bridges between the East and the West and to revere the achievements of different civilizations. These thinkers and universal citizens of the early twentieth century celebrated ideas and behaviors that transcended geographical boundaries and class distinctions, and saw the kind of enrichment that every human being benefits from when we recognize that which connects and unites us.

They wrote about how human beings are more connected to each other than they know.

They believed in the oneness of humanity and made their voices heard both in the East and in the West. That is why they wrote in both Arabic and English, and that is why they are cultural bridges and messengers of Peace.

Their place on the world stage is the result of the enlightenment they gained from their small country which values diversity and recognizes that by bringing Christians, Muslims, Druze, Jews, Bahá'ís, Buddhists and others under the same tent, conflicts diminish and the road to Peace becomes more possible.

Those dreamers of the early twentieth century inspire us and motivate us to continue on their path, a path that upholds the oneness of humanity.

However, as I mentioned earlier, what transpires on the world stage is often not about Peace. The Gibran Chair for Values and Peace, and the other two Peace Chairs within the College of Behavioral and Social Sciences at the University of Maryland, have much work to do. The challenges are tremendous. Many might say that the path to Peace is blocked or, at best, is not clear.

I believe we need to reimagine Peace, the way Nelson Mandela was able to reimagine his society even from a prison cell; the way Gandhi was able to reimagine independence even under colonial rule; the way Gibran and Rihani were able to reimagine bridges of understanding between the East and the West and in particular a cultural understanding between the Arabs and the U.S.

The Gibran Chair will be driven by a vision of the world that can reach a stage where the vast majority of individuals believe in equality for everyone regardless of race, ethnicity, religion, or gender, where the vast majority recognizes that the Other, no matter who she/he is, is a member of one's circle.

As the American poet Edwin Markham wrote:

> He drew a circle that shut me out—
> Heretic, rebel, a thing to flout.

But love and I had the wit to win:
We drew a circle and took him in.[9]

The Gibran Chair will continue to explore how humanity can draw a circle that takes in everyone.

Gibran, the Lebanese immigrant who lived in the U.S. and became a global citizen, gained wisdom and compassion for the Other, for all humans, and for the oneness of humanity.

Wise and compassionate men and women inhabit our world with the purpose of extending the hearts and minds of others.

The Gibran Chair through its academic programs will attempt to extend our hearts and minds so we can work together on advancing Peace in our global village.

---

9   Edwin Markham, "Outwitted," in *The Shoes of Happiness and Other Poems* (Garden City, NY: Doubleday, Page and Co., 1916), 1.

May Rihani gives the Inaugural Lecture. (Photo courtesy of UMD's College of Behavioral and Social Sciences)

BIBLIOGRAPHY

de Spinoza, Baruch. *Theologico-Political Treatise*. Trans. by R. H. M. Elwes. London: Routledge, 1895.

Gandhi, Mahatma and Richard Attenborough. *The Words of Gandhi*. New York: Newmarket Press, 1982.

Gibran, Kahlil. *Gibran Khalil Gibran: The Complete Works*. Comp. Tony P. Naufal. Beirut: Naufal, 2014.

Gibran, Kahlil. *The Prophet*. New York: Alfred A. Knopf, 1923.

Gibran, Kahlil. *Jesus the Son of Man*. New York: Alfred A. Knopf, 1928.

Gibran, Kahlil. *The Vision: Reflections on the Way of the Soul*. Trans. Juan R.I. Cole. London: Penguin Books, 1998.

Huntington, Samuel. *The Clash of Civilizations and the Remaking of World Order*. New York: Simon & Schuster, 1996.

Lutkehaus, Nancy. *Margaret Mead: The Making of an American Icon*. Princeton, NJ: Princeton University Press, 2008.

Mahmassani, Maher. "Secularism in Islam: A Path to Peace." Lecture delivered under the auspices of the Kahlil Gibran Chair for Values and Peace at the University of Maryland on 11 October 2016 (see go.umd.edu/Mahmassani).

Mandela, Nelson. *Long Walk to Freedom: The Autobiography of Nelson Mandela*. Boston: Little Brown, 1994.

Markham, Edwin. "Outwitted." In *The Shoes of Happiness and Other Poems*. Garden City, NY: Doubleday, Page and Co., 1916.

Rihani, Ameen Fares. *The Book of Khalid*. Brooklyn, NY: Melville House Publishing, 2012.

Rogers, Paul. *Contemporary Security Studies*. Oxford: Oxford University Press, 2007.

ADDITIONAL REMARKS

ALI KARANOUH
First Secretary and Consul
Embassy of Lebanon in Washington, D.C.

Dr. Loh, President of the University of Maryland;
Dr. Ball, Dean of the College of Behavioral and Social Sciences;
Ms. Rihani, Director of the Khalil Gibran Chair for Values and Peace;

Ladies and Gentlemen,

I am delighted to join you tonight as the representative of the Embassy of Lebanon in Washington, D.C. I join you at this important event convened in this prestigious university—the University of Maryland—that has established a Chair to pay tribute to and promote the legacy of Gibran Khalil Gibran, especially his belief in brotherhood and tolerance; his aspiration for freedom, justice and universal peace; his passion for beauty and generosity; and his call for purity, unselfishness and love.

Today, in the midst of wars, violence, corruption, exploitation, poverty, extremism, and discrimination that the East and the West are passing through, more than ever we feel the need to highlight Gibran's teachings. Gibran, who came to the U.S. from Lebanon, shared a message of peaceful coexistence and dialogue among civilizations. He believed in the unity of religions and humanity, saying: "I love you my brother whoever you are...You and I are children of one faith,...fingers of the loving hand of one supreme being, a hand extended to all."

Gibran was among the first wave of Lebanese emigrants who arrived from the mountain of Bsharri in northern Lebanon to the shores of the United States to live "The American

Dream." The challenges of his life in Lebanon—and the life he subsequently led in Boston, Paris, and New York—served as a continuing education and helped shape his great wisdom.

In my country of Lebanon, and in the Arab world generally, Gibran is regarded as one of the great figures of the *Nahda*, the Arab Renaissance. This Renaissance brought new and enlightened thinking, social modernization, and political reforms that helped the Arab world move forward to a new phase in its history. Gibran is an enlightened poet and philosopher, an advocate of human rights—especially women's rights—and a rebel against oppression and more importantly against "mental imprisonment."

I will conclude by stating that I am one who believes that ideas are the most powerful instruments—more powerful than any weapon—and I am confident that May Rihani will be a great voice promoting and amplifying Gibran's ideas and thoughts.

Thank you to the University of Maryland for honoring a great thinker from Lebanon and of the world.

First Secretary and Consul of the Lebanese Embassy in Washington Ali Karanouh delivers closing remarks. (Photo courtesy of UMD's College of Behavioral and Social Sciences)

Appendices to the Inaugural Lecture

Appendix

REFLECTIONS ON THE
INAUGURAL LECTURE

Editor's note: The brief commentaries contained in this appendix were, in their original form, sent separately and privately to May Rihani in the days following her Inaugural Lecture. Subsequently, they were collected and—with the express permission and approval of each author—edited for publication. The views expressed are strictly those of the individual authors, not the organizations with which they are affiliated.

► ◻ ◄

"This Inaugural Lecture—presented before a distinguished audience of thought leaders, policy makers, researchers, academics, and students—is inspirational, motivational, scholarly, well presented and organized (in a non-linear way), and contains a good balance of theory, policy, and realistic activism. The main text is presented together with two supplemental brochures that are beautifully crafted, aesthetic, content-oriented, highly informative, and enlightening."

— **Leonard G. Epstein**, former Senior Adviser on Culture, Language and Health Literacy with the Health Resources and Services Administration, United States Department of Health and Human Services

►□◄

"In her inaugural lecture, May Rihani articulates both a vision of peace and a realistic framework for implementation. She grounds her analysis theoretically within the peace models literature. The great achievement of this text is that she seamlessly and convincingly establishes peace, justice and equity as inseparable and interdependent—naming their reach and linking them to issues of inclusivity and the seldom acknowledged centrality of the skill and attribute of active listening."

— **Patricia Flederman**, International Education Consultant

►□◄

"By sharing a hybrid perspective grounded in both contemporary academic peace research and timeless humanistic traditions, May Rihani has engineered a unique intellectual compass that can help guide faculty and students working toward the realization of peace in the twenty-first century. Her vision is clear, creative, bold, and powerful."

— **Stacy J. Kosko**, Assistant Research Professor at the Center for International Development and Conflict Management (CIDCM), University of Maryland

► □ ◄

"This wonderful lecture by May Rihani expresses all the most important ideas people should be thinking about in terms of peace and building a better world."

— **Carolyn Long**, former Vice President of Interaction

► □ ◄

"Brilliantly delivered on the eve of the United Nations International Day of Peace, May Rihani's talk should be circulated and read widely."

— **Jerome Glenn**, CEO, The Millennium Project

► □ ◄

"May Rihani's speech establishes her as a leading advocate of peace, and one well suited to bridge the academic world of ideas and the policy world of action. Clearly, she is determined to make a difference and motivates her readers to do the same."

— **Massoud Maalouf**, former Lebanese ambassador to Canada, Poland and Chile

►▫◄

"May Rihani's talk is energizing, broadening, and challenging. While listening to her words, I was moved to think back to my own experiences working for the U.S. Government and in international development in places like the East German border in the 1970s, Zimbabwe in the 1980s, and Uganda in the 1990s. During those times, I witnessed what can only be described as pure evil, perpetrated by certain political systems and individuals. For me, those experiences showed definite limits on both dialogue and realistic options for peace. Yet, I was heartened by May Rihani's insightful presentation because it provides a basis for a new, worldly optimism—throwing important light on a path to peace we can all strive for."

— **Kurt D. Moses**, Director, Policy and Information Systems, Global Learning, FHI360 (formerly Family Health International)

►▫◄

"This unique and inspired Inaugural Lecture by May Rihani of the Kahlil Gibran Chair for Values and Peace outlines a powerful and realistic agenda for building bridges of understanding and peace in the world."

— **Kent Davis-Packard**, Adjunct Professor of Middle East Studies and American Foreign Policy, Johns Hopkins School of Advanced International Studies (SAIS)

►▫◄

"May Rihani's incisive analysis, which prompted a rare standing ovation in a university setting, makes the connection between peace and gender equity. Her lecture also underlines the centrality of values—such as recognizing our commonalities—to peace."

— **Elaine Murphy**, visiting scholar with The Population Bureau and former professor of Public Health, George Washington University

►▫◄

"Through her inspirational words, May Rihani instills her audience with hope that thoughtful, diligent dialogue and active, cooperative engagement can promote peace within individuals, between communities, and among peoples. Her lecture challenges us to begin by seeking peace within ourselves, at the deepest level. Thereafter, May Rihani demonstrates how a focus on peace can permeate all we see and do, from the small personal interactions of our lives to the opportunities we have to make a difference in the larger world that is so in need of the peace we can each bring to bear."

— **Sandy Oleksy-Ojikutu**, PhD, Senior Education Advisor in the Bureau for Africa, U.S. Agency for International Development

►▫◄

"Weaving together diverse concepts and practices drawn from many disciplines, May Rihani has created a multi-layered, complex, and innovative intellectual tapestry that will guide the vital peace-building work of the Kahlil Gibran Chair in the coming years."

— **Cecilia Perry**, Attorney

►▫◄

"May Rihani's Inaugural Lecture as the Director of the George and Lisa Zakhem Kahlil Gibran Chair for Values and Peace will find a ready readership among the peace community and scholars studying the dynamics of conflict resolution and conflict management. Additionally, the policy community— such as faculty and students of the National Defense University, USAID staff, and Foreign Service Officers— should actively engage the ideas and perspectives contained in this groundbreaking lecture."

— **Nancy Pielemeier**, former Vice President of Abt Associates

►▫◄

"Albert Einstein said that 'imagination is more important than knowledge,' and in her Inaugural Lecture May Rihani urges us not only to apply the world's existing knowledge but also to imagine new and creative solutions to major problems of peace. She is eminently qualified to lead the Gibran Chair in its mission to empower individuals and institutions and to enliven a cooperative pursuit of peace. In re-launching the Chair, Ms. Rihani earned the support of the Arab-American community and merits assistance from all participants in the global movement toward understanding and peace."

— **Diana M. Richards**, Arts Programming Consultant and former U.S. Foreign Service Officer

►▫◄

"Readers of May Rihani's auspicious lecture will discover inspiring ideas rooted in an expansive agenda that is a genuine call to action."

— **Katherine F. Russell**, Associate Dean of the College of Behavioral and Social Sciences, University of Maryland

►▫◄

"May Rihani's remarks make us aware that women are half the population, not a special interest group. She does so while advocating the concept of building bridges, a metaphor for the kind of 'reaching out' that is so critical in today's world. Rather than pointing fingers at 'the other' and focusing on negativity, May Rihani argues that the way forward to peace is by drawing a circle that encompasses everyone."

— **Cathie Saadeh**, Attorney

►▫◄

"In her incisive and ambitious Inaugural Lecture, May Rihani honors the work of her distinguished predecessor—Professor Suheil Bushrui—while also laying out a bold agenda that will take the Gibran Chair in new and vitally important directions."

— **Paul A. Shackel**, Professor and Chair of the Department of Anthropology, University of Maryland

►▫◄

"May Rihani's astute remarks are a unique celebration of humankind infused with hope, optimism, and a 'can do' spirit."

— **Eliot Sorel**, Senior Scholar in Healthcare Innovation and Policy Research, George Washington University School of Medicine and School of Public Health

►▫◄

"May Rihani's Inaugural Lecture at the University of Maryland's Kahlil Gibran Chair for Values and Peace is a masterful roadmap of the most thoughtful approaches to building peace in a turbulent world, ranging from mobilizing women's empowerment and leadership, to bringing together academics and practitioners within an open architecture of learning. Proponents of the ideals of global citizenship will find inspiration in the guiding principles that May Rihani so ambitiously defines. The author merits a heartfelt thank you for brilliant leadership and realistic proposals to meet the key challenges of our time."

— **Doaa Taha**, Chair of the Women's Empowerment Forum of the American-Arab Anti Discrimination Committee, Senior Vice President of Grey Matter Int. (GMI), and Professor of Analytics at Harrisburg University of Science and Technology

EVENT PHOTOS

Professor Marilyn Merritt of George Washington University and May Rihani before the Inaugural Lecture proceedings. (Photo courtesy of Marilyn Merritt)

Audience members, including (left to right) Dr. David Backer, Dr. Tom Merrick, President Wallace Loh, Dr. Elaine Murphy, Professor Peter Wien, and Cecilia Perry, Esq., listen to the Inaugural Lecture. (Photo courtesy of UMD's College of Behavioral and Social Sciences)

May Rihani (at podium) and members of the audience. (Photo courtesy of UMD's College of Behavioral and Social Sciences)

Former Vice President of Interaction, Carolyn Long (left), and Senior Vice President Emeritus of Management Systems International, Marina Fanning. (Photo courtesy of UMD's College of Behavioral and Social Sciences)

Janet Maalouf, wife of former Lebanese Ambassador to Canada Massoud Maalouf, speaks with Dean Gregory Ball. (Photo courtesy of UMD's College of Behavioral and Social Sciences)

(Left to right) President Wallace Loh, Dean Gregory Ball, and First Secretary and Consul of the Lebanese Embassy in Washington Ali Karanouh confer prior to the Inaugural Lecture. (Photo courtesy of UMD's College of Behavioral and Social Sciences)

President Wallace Loh addresses the audience. (Photo courtesy of UMD's College of Behavioral and Social Sciences)

Ali Karanouh and May Rihani. (Photo courtesy of UMD's College of Behavioral and Social Sciences)

Dean Gregory Ball addresses the audience. (Photo courtesy of UMD's College of Behavioral and Social Sciences)

University of Maryland President Wallace Loh. (Photo courtesy of UMD's College of Behavioral and Social Sciences)

Inaugural Lecture Proceedings (pamphlet)

——— THE GEORGE AND LISA ZAKHEM ———

Kahlil Gibran Chair

——— FOR VALUES AND PEACE ———

INAUGURAL LECTURE

*Global Interconnections, Several Paths to Peace:
The Vision and Programs of the Gibran Chair*

by

Ms. May A. Rihani

organized by

The College of Behavioral and Social Sciences

and

**The George and Lisa Zakhem Kahlil Gibran Chair for
Values and Peace**

in association with

The Embassy of Lebanon in Washington, D.C.

Tuesday, September 20, 2016   Welcome 6:30pm
College Park Marriott Inn & Conference Center   Lecture and Dinner 7:00pm

PROGRAM

MASTER OF CEREMONIES
Dr. Gregory Ball
Dean, College of Behavioral and Social Sciences

WELCOMING REMARKS
Dr. Wallace Loh
President, University of Maryland

INTRODUCTORY REMARKS
Dean Gregory Ball

DINNER

INTRODUCING THE INAUGURAL LECTURE SPEAKER
Dean Gregory Ball

INAUGURAL LECTURE
Ms. May A. Rihani
Director, Kahlil Gibran Chair

Global Interconnections, Several Paths to Peace:
The Vision and Programs of the Gibran Chair

BRIEF REMARKS
Mr. Ali Karanouh
First Secretary and Consul
Embassy of Lebanon in Washington, D.C.

CLOSING REMARKS
Dean Gregory Ball

DESSERT

GIBRAN

Kahlil Gibran is a Lebanese-American writer born in 1883 to a Maronite family in Bsharri in northern Lebanon. He lived in Lebanon until the age of twelve.

In 1895, he migrated to the United States with his mother; his younger sisters, Mariana and Sultana; and his elder half-brother, Butrus. Gibran's mother, along with Butrus, wanted Gibran to absorb more of his own heritage. Thus, at the age of 15, Gibran returned to Lebanon to study at Al-Hikma, a preparatory school and higher-education institute in Beirut. He started a student literary magazine with a classmate and was elected as "college poet." He stayed in Lebanon for several years before returning to Boston in 1902.

Gibran held his first art exhibition of his drawings in 1904 in Boston, at Day's studio. During this exhibition, Gibran met Mary Haskell, a respected headmistress ten years his senior. The two formed an important friendship that lasted the rest of Gibran's life. Though publicly discreet, their correspondence reveals an exalted intimacy. Haskell influenced not only Gibran's personal life, but also his career. She became Gibran's confidante, patron and benefactor. Thanks to the generous sponsorship of Haskell, in 1908, Gibran went to study art in Paris for two years, and then returned to Boston in 1910.

On the advice of his friend and fellow Lebanese emigre writer Ameen Rihani, Gibran moved to New York in 1912 where he became the leading member of the Pen League, also known as Al-Rabita Al-Kalamiya, alongside important Lebanese-American authors such as Rihani and Naimy. These Lebanese-American authors became the progenitors of the Arab intellectual Renaissance.

In 1923, Gibran published The Prophet, which many believe was influenced by Christianity, especially on the topic of spiritual love, and also by his mysticism that is the result of a convergence of several different influences: Christianity, Islam, Sufism, Hinduism and theosophy.

Although Gibran spent most of his life in the US, his attachment to Lebanon, his homeland – reinforced by the time spent at Al-Hikmah in Beirut – remained strong and vital to the end of his life. Symbolic of his attachment to Lebanon was his lifelong correspondence with the Lebanese writer, May Ziadah. Though the two never met, a sentimental, but platonic, attachment developed between them.

Gibran died at the age of 48 in New York City in 1931. He had expressed the wish that he be buried in Lebanon. This wish was fulfilled in 1932, when Mary Haskell and his sister Mariana purchased the Mar Sarkis Monastery in Lebanon, which became the Gibran Museum.

GEORGE AND LISA ZAKHEM
KAHLIL GIBRAN CHAIR
FOR VALUES AND PEACE

The George and Lisa Zakhem Kahlil Gibran Chair for Values and Peace is one of the College of Behavioral and Social Sciences' three endowed Peace Chairs at the University of Maryland, College Park, and is an endowed academic program that strengthens understanding between Eastern and Western cultures in general, and the Arab ethos and American values in particular.

The famous Lebanese writer Kahlil Gibran dedicated his life and works to demonstrating the importance of universal values, the interconnectedness of religions, common ground among cultures, the importance of dialogue, and the goodness of humanity as a whole. He believed the more we explore our interconnectedness as humans, the more we understand and respect the universal values that underpin different cultures. Gibran wrote about and advocated for social justice, freedoms, equality, unity and peace.

The Gibran Chair's active program addresses major global topics such as: Studying the Pursuit of Peace; Exploring Paths toward Peace; Examining Common Ground; Understanding Cultural Pluralism; Highlighting the Contributions of Women toward Peace; Deepening Cross-Cultural Understanding; Transcending the Barriers of East and West; Revisiting Poetry, Literature and Art as Connectors within the Global Village; and Celebrating Universal Values. This program will be implemented through research, lectures, seminars, workshops, symposia, conferences and academic publications.

THE GEORGE AND LISA ZAKHEM
Kahlil Gibran Chair
FOR VALUES AND PEACE

COLLEGE OF
BEHAVIORAL &
SOCIAL SCIENCES

GIBRAN AND FRIENDS
(PAMPHLET)

—— THE GEORGE AND LISA ZAKHEM ——

Kahlil Gibran Chair

—— FOR VALUES AND PEACE ——

GIBRAN AND FRIENDS

Gibran and the Circle of Individuals
Who Were Important in His Life

presented on the occasion of the
Inaugural Lecture

Tuesday, September 20, 2016
College Park Marriott Inn & Conference Center

1 - Gibran
1883-1931

Author of *The Prophet*. Gibran and other émigré writers founded the New York Pen League in 1916. He is the third best-selling writer of all time, after Shakespeare and Lao-Tzu.

2 - Mary Haskell
1873-1964

Gibran's benefactress and editor. A strong relationship developed between Gibran and Mary, as attested in their intense and loving correspondence.

3 - Ameen Rihani
1876-1940

A Lebanese émigré author who is considered the Father of Arab-American Literature. Gibran called him *mou'allimi*, 'my teacher'. Their correspondence focused on key issues that characterize the Arab Literary Renaissance of the early 20th century.

4 - May Ziadeh
1886-1941

A Lebanese writer who lived in both Lebanon and Egypt. She and Gibran maintained an extensive written correspondence though they never met. Their correspondence lasted nineteen years until his death in 1931.

5 - Mikhail Naimy
1889-1988

A Lebanese émigré author who, with Gibran and eight other authors, formed the New York Pen League. This group launched the rebirth of Arabic Literature.

6 - Elia Abou Madi
1890-1957

A Lebanese émigré poet and member of the New York Pen League. He worked with a number of Arab-American writers, including Gibran.

7 - Naoum Mokarzel
1864-1932

A Lebanese émigré who founded *Al-Hoda*, one of the first Arabic newspapers in the US, and became an influential publisher. *Al-Hoda* became the largest Arabic daily in the US and many of Gibran's early Arabic articles appeared in it.

8 - Alfred Knopf
1892-1984

An American publisher who published *The Prophet* in 1925.

9 - Josephine Preston Peabody
1874-1922

An American poet who had an intellectual friendship with Gibran. The title of Gibran's greatest work, *The Prophet*, may well be due to Peabody's suggestions. When she saw an early manuscript in 1903 she

said it was a "prophetic text" and referred to Gibran as "my young prophet."

10 - Fred Holland Day
1864-1933

An avant-garde American artist and photographer who taught photography in Boston. The 13-year-old Gibran was one of his students. It is said that the early drawings of Gibran were influenced by Holland Day's photography.

11 - Auguste Rodin
1840-1917

Gibran met Rodin in the sculptor's studio in Paris. Gibran called him the Great. After visiting Rodin at his studio Gibran wrote a poem titled "Man the Creator."

12 - Yussef Al-Howayek
1883-1962

Lebanese painter and sculptor who befriended Gibran in Paris between 1908 and 1910 when Gibran was studying at Parisian art studios. The two of them and Ameen Rihani spent time together in Paris thinking about how to influence Lebanon's future.

13 - Abdul Massih Haddad
1888-1963

A Syrian born émigré writer and a member of the New York Pen League. He was publisher of the literary journal *Al-Sayeh*.

14 - Marianna Gibran
1884-1972

Gibran's sister who, following the death of their mother and in the absence of their father, devoted her life to her brother. She worked as a seamstress to support them.

15 - Kamileh Rahmeh-Gibran
1853-1903

Gibran's mother, who decided to migrate to the US with her four children: Boutros, Gibran's half-brother; Marianna and Sultana, Gibran's sisters; and Gibran. Kamileh was the sole supporter of the family of five during their first years in Boston.

16 - Nasib Arida
1887-1946

A Syrian born émigré poet and writer and a member of the New York Pen League. He was publisher of the literary journal *Al-Founoun*.

17 - Louise Imogen Guiney
1861-1920

An Irish-American poet and essayist who was a close friend of Fred Holland Day and became a friend of Gibran in the early years of the 20th century.

18 - Andrew Ghareeb
1898-2000

A Lebanese émigré translator who was given permission by Gibran in 1929 to translate his Arabic writings into English.

19 - Barbara Young
1879-1961

An American literary critic active during the 1920s. She met Gibran in New York

City in 1926. She became his secretary and companion until the end of his life.

20 - Alexander and Marjorie Morten
met Gibran in 1913

American pioneering patrons of contemporary art who encouraged Gibran, ar-ranged for American painters to visit his studio, and who bought many of his draw-ings and paintings.

21 - Albert Pinkham Ryder
1847-1917

An American painter best known for his poetic and moody allegorical works. Gibran admired his work and wrote him a poem that was published in 1915.

22 - Ayub Tabet
1884-1951

A Lebanese who was one of Gibran's best friends during his years at *Al-Hikmah* in Beirut. Gibran admired the fact that Tabet became a political activist against the Ot-toman Empire, and was elected president of the League of Liberation.

23 - Charlotte Teller
1876-1953

An American novelist, playwright, suffragette, and freelance writer for Hearst pub-lications. She was a close friend of Gibran, Mary Haskell, and Ameen Rihani.

24 - Emilie Michel, aka Micheline
1889-1931

A young French teacher at the school where Mary Haskell was the principal. She was introduced to Gibran by Haskell and then became his model.

25 - Emile Zaidan
early 20th century

A Lebanese publisher who lived in Cairo. He was the editor-in-chief of *Al-Hilal*, a cultural and literary magazine that published many of Gibran's Arabic poems and articles.

—— THE GEORGE AND LISA ZAKHEM ——
Kahlil Gibran Chair
—— FOR VALUES AND PEACE ——

COLLEGE OF
BEHAVIORAL &
SOCIAL SCIENCES

SUPPLEMENTARY MATERIAL

Notes on the Life and Works of Kahlil Gibran

Kahlil Gibran was a product of Lebanon and the United States and his life and works serve as a bridge between the East and the West. This brief survey provides notes on this universal author and artist who continues to inspire millions.

Kahlil Gibran was born on January 6, 1883 in Bsharri in northern Lebanon. He lived in Lebanon until the age of twelve.

In 1895, he migrated to the United States with his mother Kamle, his younger sisters Marianna and Sultana, and his elder half-brother, Boutros. The Gibrans settled in Boston's South End, which at the time hosted the second-largest Lebanese-American community in the United States.

His mother began working as a seamstress peddler, selling lace and linens. Gibran started school on September 30, 1895 and was placed in a special class for immigrants so he could learn English. Gibran also enrolled in an art school at a nearby settlement house. He developed a serious interest in literature, drawing, and painting during his school years.

Gibran's mother, along with Boutros, wanted Gibran to learn Arabic and experience his heritage, so at the age of fifteen they sent him back to Lebanon to study at Al-Hikma, a preparatory school and higher education institute in Beirut. At Al-Hikma, he started a student literary magazine with a classmate and was elected as college poet.

Gibran remained in Lebanon for several years before re-turning to Boston in 1902. Two weeks before he arrived back, his sister Sultana died of tuberculosis at the age of fourteen. The next year, Boutros died of the same disease and his mother died of cancer. Gibran and his sister Marianna were the only

Two images of Gibran's hometown: Bsharri, Lebanon. (Photos courtesy of Mr. Ziad Rahme)

Gibran during his childhood years (Image courtesy of the Gibran National Committee)

two left from the family of five. Marianna supported herself and her brother by working at a dressmaker's shop.

Gibran held the first exhibition of his drawings in 1904 in Boston, at Fred Holland Day's studio. During this exhibition, Gibran met Mary Elizabeth Haskell, a respected headmistress ten years his senior. The two formed an important friendship that lasted for the rest of Gibran's life. Meeting Haskel might have been the most impactful event in his life. Their friendship, though publicly discreet, became an anchor for Gibran. Their correspondence reveals the importance of her presence in his life: she influenced not only Gibran's personal life, but also his career. She became Gibran's confidante, editor, advisor, patron, and benefactor.

Gibran began writing in Arabic and his first book, *Al-Musiqah* ("Music") was published in 1905. He continued to write in Arabic and published *Ara'is al-Muruj* ("Nymphs of the Valley"), in which he was critical of the relationship between the church and state and advocated their separation. He then published *Al-Arwah al Mutamarridah* ("Spirits Rebellious") in 1908, which reaffirmed his rebellion against a strong relationship between secular and religious institutions. He also published *Al-Ajniha al-Mutakassira* ("Broken Wings") in 1912, based on his personal love experience in Lebanon, and then *Dam'a wa Ibtisama* ("A Tear and a Smile") in 1914.

During the first years of the twentieth century, Gibran became increasingly interested in art and wanted to continue to study drawing and painting. Thanks to the generous sponsorship of Mary Haskell, in 1908 Gibran went to Paris to study art for two years. While there, he met a fellow art student who became a lifelong friend, Youssef Huwayyik. Gibran returned to Boston in 1910.

On the advice of his friend and fellow Lebanese emigre writer Ameen Rihani, Gibran moved to New York in 1912. He continued writing and publishing in Arabic until 1918. That year he also published his first book in English, *The Madman*, a brief volume written in a style that could be considered poetry or poetic prose.

The Pen League, also known as *Al Rabita Al Qalamiya*, was the first Arab-American literary society. The Pen League was initially formed in 1915, and subsequently re-formed in 1920 by a group of Lebanese-American and Syrian-American writers living in New York. Gibran became the leading member of the Pen League, alongside important Lebanese-American authors such as Ameen Rihani, Elia Abu Madi and Mikhail Naimy, and few Syrian-American writers including Abdul Massih Haddad and Nassib Arida. These authors became the leading figures of a movement which has been called the Arab Renaissance.

In 1923, Gibran published *The Prophet*, which was the result of many influences including Christianity, especially on the topic of spiritual love. *The Prophet* demonstrates how mysticism shaped Gibran's life and how his interpretation of mysticism was influenced by his understanding of the common ground among Christianity, Islam, Sufism, and Hinduism.

The Prophet is composed of 26 poetic essays and its success was unprecedented. The work won Gibran universal recognition, becoming extremely popular in the U.S. during the counterculture of the 1960s. Gibran is the third best-selling poet of all time, after Shakespeare and Lao-Tzu. Since its publication, *The Prophet* has never been out of print. *The Prophet* is translated into more than 40 languages, and was one of the bestselling books of the twentieth century in the United States.

Gibran's health, never very good, started deteriorating in the mid 1920s, yet he continued to write and publish in English. He published *Sand and Foam* in 1926, *Jesus, Son of Man* in 1928, and *The Earth Gods* in 1931.

Although Gibran spent most of his life in the U.S., his attachment to his homeland of Lebanon was reinforced by the time spent at Al-Hikmah in Beirut between 1898 and 1901. His link with Lebanon remained strong and vital to the end of his life. This attachment to Lebanon appears in many of his articles and essays. A possible manifestation of his attachment to Lebanon might be found in his lifelong correspondence with the Lebanese writer, May Ziadeh. Although, the two never met, a serious, extensive and powerful written communication took place between them, and their letters are filled with special expressions to each other and are witness to their unique relationship, their transparent openness, and their passionate commitment to art and literature.

Gibran died at the age of 48 in New York City on April 10, 1931.

Before his death, Gibran expressed his wish to be buried in Lebanon. This request was fulfilled in 1932, when Mary Haskell and his sister Marianna purchased the Mar Sarkis Monastery in Lebanon, which has since become the Gibran Museum as well as his final resting place.

By the staff of the George and Lisa Zakhem Kahlil Gibran Chair for Values and Peace

Kahlil Gibran (Image courtesy of the Gibran National Committee)

May A. Rihani Biography

May Rihani serves as Director of the George and Lisa Zakhem Gibran Chair for Values and Peace at the University of Maryland, a position she was appointed to in May 2016.

Before joining the University of Maryland, May served as Senior Vice President at FHI360, the Academy for Educational Development (AED), and Creative Associates International. Her responsibilities included ensuring the planning and implementation of educational reform projects as well as integrating gender perspectives into these programs. She designed, planned, and managed numerous educational reform projects as well as cross-cutting gender programs and girls' education projects in Afghanistan, Benin, Congo (DRC), Egypt, El Salvador, Ghana, Guinea, Jordan, Kenya, Malawi, Mali, Morocco, Niger, Pakistan, Qatar, Saudi Arabia, Tanzania, Tunisia, Uganda, and Yemen.

As a result of her international work, May was elected to serve as Co-Chair of the United Nations Girls' Education Initiative (UNGEI) from 2008 to 2010.

May's expertise in education and gender equity attracted the attention of many professional experts in development and donor organizations, who sought to enlist her ideas and analytical skills to aid their efforts. She succeeded after a few years in expanding the donor base of the Center for Gender Equity (at AED) to include not just traditional donors—such as USAID and the World Bank—but also the Asia Development Bank, the

Netherlands AID, the British international assistance agency (DFID), UNICEF, UNFPA, as well as several private foundations.

Ms. Rihani's extensive work in girls' education includes research, policy assessments, innovative program designs, training, systems analysis, and management of country programs. She presented lessons learned, best practices, and strategies on girls' education at numerous international conferences and symposia. Ms. Rihani is also a leading voice internationally on the relationship between girls' education and health nutrition, reproductive health, and economic productivity.

Drawing on her work with the ministries of education and civil society in many African, Middle Eastern, and Asian countries to advance basic education and girls' education, Ms. Rihani wrote many reports and several books. One of her publications is *Learning for the 21st Century: Girls' Education in the Middle East and North Africa*. This publication has been translated into French, Arabic, and Farsi. Her most recent technical publication is *Keeping the Promise: Five Benefits of Girls' Secondary Education*.

In addition, May Rihani is a bilingual author with five books in English and three in Arabic. Her latest work is a memoir entitled *Cultures Without Borders: From Beirut to Washington, D.C.* (Authors House, 2014).

Dr. Kathy Barks of the University of Maryland Honors College and May Rihani. (Photo courtesy of UMD's College of Behavioral and Social Sciences)

About the Gibran Chair

The George and Lisa Zakhem Kahlil Gibran Chair for Values and Peace at the College of Behavioral and Social Sciences of the University of Maryland is an endowed academic program that strengthens understanding between Eastern and Western cultures in general, and the Arab ethos and American values in particular.

The famous Lebanese poet and scholar Kahlil Gibran dedicated his life and works to demonstrating the importance of universal values, the interconnectedness of religions, common ground among cultures, the importance of dialogue, and the goodness of humanity as a whole. He believed the more we explore our interconnectedness as humans, the more we understand and respect the universal values that underpin different cultures. Gibran wrote about and advocated for social justice, freedoms, equality, unity, and peace. The legacy left by Kahlil Gibran deserves to be highlighted, celebrated, and reinforced. It can serve as an inspiration to students, scholars, professors, and policy makers. It can strengthen the belief that Peace is possible.

Director May Rihani joined the Gibran Chair in May 2016, and works to expand upon and add to the legacy and foundation created by the Chair's first incumbent, Professor Suheil Bushrui.

The Gibran Chair's active program addresses major global topics such as:

- Studying the Pursuit of Peace;
- Exploring Paths towards Peace;
- Examining Common Ground;
- Understanding Cultural Pluralism;
- Highlighting the Contributions of Women towards Peace;
- Deepening Cross-Cultural Understanding;
- Transcending the Barriers of East and West;
- Revisiting Poetry, Literature and Art as Connectors within the Global Village; and
- Celebrating Universal Values.

This program is implemented through research, lectures, seminars, workshops, symposia, conferences, and academic publications. In addition, Director May Rihani teaches a University of Maryland Honors College course that resonates with the vision and spirit of the Gibran Chair.

The Gibran Chair is one of the College of Behavioral and Social Sciences' three endowed Peace Chairs. The three chairs are committed to the innovative pursuit of global peace and understanding. Through their research, programming, and the inspiring and globally renowned speakers they bring to the University of Maryland, BSOS's Peace Chairs work to be the solution to the world's great challenges.

May Rihani closes the Inaugural Lecture proceedings by thanking audience members for their participation. (Photo courtesy of UMD's College of Behavioral and Social Sciences)

SUPPORTING THE GIBRAN CHAIR

The George and Lisa Zakhem Kahlil Gibran Chair for Values and Peace is an endowed academic program that strengthens understanding between Eastern and Western cultures in general, and the complementarity of Arab and American values in particular. The Gibran Chair is one of the College of Behavioral and Social Sciences' three endowed peace chairs. These chairs are each dedicated to the innovative pursuit of global peace and understanding. Through their research, programming and the inspiring and globally renowned speakers they bring to the University of Maryland, BSOS's Peace Chairs work to be the solution to the world's great challenges.

Contributions provide valuable support to Gibran Chair lectures, publications, workshops, symposia, conferences, and other initiatives. For more information on the George and Lisa Zakhem Kahlil Gibran Chair for Values and Peace please visit: Gibranchair.umd.edu

For information on giving to the Gibran Chair's Operating Fund or Endowment, please visit go.umd.edu/SupportGibran-Chair or contact the Gibran Chair at tel. 301-405-3711.

NOTES

www.ingramcontent.com/pod-product-compliance
Lightning Source LLC
Chambersburg PA
CBHW060513280326

41933CB00014B/2943